PLANTS & GARDENS

BROOKLYN BOTANIC GARDEN RECORD

Hollies
A Gardener's Guide

1993

PUBLISHED IN COOPERATION WITH THE HOLLY SOCIETY OF AMERICA

Plants & Gardens, Brooklyn Botanic Garden Record (ISSN 0362-5850)

is published quarterly at 1000 Washington Ave., Brooklyn, N.Y. 11225, by the **Brooklyn Botanic Garden, Inc.**

Subscription included in Botanic Garden membership dues ($25.00 per year).

ISBN # 0-945352-79-4

Brooklyn Botanic Garden

STAFF FOR THIS EDITION:

ALAN D. COOK, GUEST EDITOR

HAROLD L. ELMORE, TECHNICAL EDITOR, HOLLY SOCIETY OF AMERICA

HERMAN C. GEHNRICH, ADVISOR/LIAISON, HOLLY SOCIETY OF AMERICA

BARBARA B. PESCH, DIRECTOR OF PUBLICATIONS

JANET MARINELLI, EDITOR

AND THE EDITORIAL COMMITTEE OF THE BROOKLYN BOTANIC GARDEN

BEKKA LINDSTROM, ART DIRECTOR

JUDITH D. ZUK, PRESIDENT, BROOKLYN BOTANIC GARDEN

ELIZABETH SCHOLTZ, DIRECTOR EMERITUS, BROOKLYN BOTANIC GARDEN

STEPHEN K-M. TIM, VICE PRESIDENT, SCIENCE & PUBLICATIONS

FRONT AND BACK COVER: PHOTOGRAPHS BY PAMELA HARPER

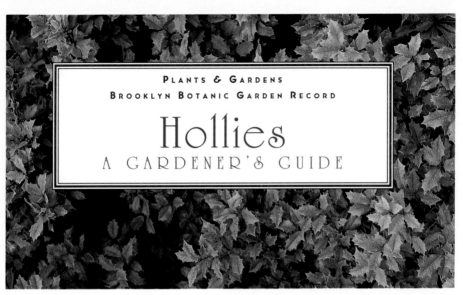

PLANTS & GARDENS
BROOKLYN BOTANIC GARDEN RECORD

Hollies
A GARDENER'S GUIDE

VOL. 49, NO. 2, SUMMER 1993

HANDBOOK #135

Introduction

olly is woven into the lore and legend, romance and religion, medicine and music and rites and rituals of many peoples on at least four continents and a bunch of islands.

Today, few in this country brew holly tea or other holly beverages. Midnight dances around moonlit holly trees are infrequent.

Instead, we use holly in the landscape in myriad ways; we train dwarfish hollies into bonsai; we work holly into wreaths and other arrangements.

The increasing interest in holly, both the evergreen and the new deciduous varieties, prompted the production of this handbook.

Frederick Douglass wrote in 1876, "If there is no struggle, there is no progress."

The struggle is accomplished. And it could not have been accomplished without the help of the Holly Society of America and the efforts of the following holly experts:

Harry William Dengler	T.R. Dudley
Michael Ecker	G.K. Eisenbeiss
Fred Galle	Dorothy B. Grosse
Gordon Jones	Patricia Joseph
E. Elizabeth Kassab	William N. Kuhl,
Richard Lawson	Virginia Morell
Dr. Elwin R. Orton Jr.	Matthew C. Perry
Robert C. Simpson	Carl W. Suk
Alice Wieman	John Wieman

To them our heart-felt thanks.

As for progress, if one reader, just one, learns something about the genus *Ilex* and/or gains pleasure from this book — that is *not* enough! So much love and other good stuff went into this book that we expect thousands of people to learn about holly and be happy about holly.

To wit, we've avoided technical terminology and arcane jargon as much as possible, though for the sake of top-shelf accuracy, they occur sometimes. Case in point: the sexually reproductive plant part of a (female) holly, botanically correctly, is a fruit. Ultimately correctly, it is a bacco drupe. Often in these pages the thing is called a berry, and we all know what it is without feeling sophomoric about it.

This book is by holly people, for holly people and for people who may wish to be holly people. The "bys" have written; the "fors" may now read. Please.

Heigh ho!

ALAN D. COOK
Guest Editor

ALAN D. COOK *is Director of Extended Services at the Dawes Arboretum in Newark, Ohio.*

American holly, *Ilex opaca*, is a hardy evergreen native to the eastern United States. It can grow to 50 feet tall or more. Its abundant, berrylike fruits come in all shades of red and orange as well as yellow.

What Makes a Holly a Holly?

W hen most gardeners think of hollies, they think of the American, English, Chinese and Japanese shrubs and trees that adorn parks and gardens. Yet hollies are widely scattered around the world, in both temperate and tropical regions of both hemispheres, and are native to every continent except Antarctica. There are between twenty and thirty species in North America alone. Most hollies occur naturally as trees and shrubs, but there are also a few climbers and epiphytes.

A number of hollies are known as "caffeine hollies" because indigenous peoples where these species are native infuse the leaves to brew a beverage that has a stimulating effect. Probably the most famous of these is yerba maté, made from *Ilex paraguariensis*, a tree native to subtropical forests of Paraguay, Argentina and Brazil. When Europeans first arrived in the Southeast, they discovered that a tea made from the leaves of the yaupon holly, *I. vomitoria*, was made by Native Americans along the Atlantic and Gulf coasts from Virginia to Texas.

All hollies fall into two broad categories: evergreen, those that retain their leaves throughout the year, and deciduous, those that lose all of their leaves during the dormant season. Gardeners have been singing the praises of the evergreen types for centuries. In recent years the deciduous hollies have begun to come into their own. With waxy fruits in shades of red, orange and yellow that cover the naked branches and persist for weeks, these plants are stars in the winter garden.

Hollies differ widely in their physical characteristics. Plant breeders have taken advantage of this variation to produce hundreds of new cultivars and hybrids.

American holly
in fruit

A spring
flowering branch

STEVE BUCHANAN

Flower cluster
in leaf axil

Flowers

Holly flowers are usually dioecious, meaning that male and female flowers are on separate plants. The flowers are white, cream, green, pink or lavender. There are usually four sepals, petals and stamens; sometimes five to nine. Flowers are borne in leaf axils, never at branch tips.

Fruit

Holly "berries" are technically globe-shaped or egg-shaped (ovate) drupes, usually made up of 4 segments, each containing one seed. Like the flowers from which they develop, they are always found in leaf axils. Today, hollies are available with white, cream, yellow, orange, red or black fruits.

Leaf

Holly leaves are always simple, never compound or lobed. They're arranged alternately (very rarely oppositely) on the stem. The leaves are leathery (coriaceous) or paperlike (chartaceous or membraneous) in texture.

WHAT'S IN A NAME?

In Denmark, holly is called "stikpalme"; in France, "le houx"; in Germany, "Christdorn" or "hultz"; in Holland, "schubbig hardkelk"; in Italy, "agrifolio"; in Spain, "acebo"; and in Wales, "celyn." But in all countries, botanists recognize the plant when it is called *Ilex*. That's just one reason why botanical names are so important.

Ilex is the name of the genus (a closely related group of plants) to which all hollies belong — well over 400 species worldwide. The species is the basic unit in plant classification. The botanical name of a plant consists of two words: the first is the genus (in this case *Ilex*), and the second is the name of the particular species (*Ilex opaca* or American holly, for example).

Further divisions below the rank of species are subspecies, varieties, forma and cultivars. Subspecies, varieties and forma occur in the wild. A cultivar is a plant specially selected or bred for horticultural use; it is usually reproduced by asexual, or vegetative, means. All holly cultivars are asexually reproduced from one parent plant and are genetically identical — which means they are clones as well as cultivars. At this level, classifications are made based upon one or more distinguishing characteristics within the species — for example, unusual leaf size or coloration. The name of the cultivar follows the name of the species in single quotes, as in *Ilex opaca* 'Canary', which is distinguished by its yellow fruit.

Longstalk holly
showing leaves
arranged alternately
on the branch and fruit in leaf axils.

Leaf Outline

Holly leaves come in a variety of shapes, from quadrangular to lanceolate (lance-shaped; several times longer than broad and widest below the middle) to oblanceolate (broadest width above the middle) to oblong or ovate.

Leaf Margin

The character of the leaf margins or edges also ranges widely from entire (without toothing or division) to dentate (toothed) to serrate (saw-toothed, with the teeth pointing toward the leaf tip) to crenate (scalloped, with shallow, rounded teeth) to spiny or any combination of the above.

Leaf Tip

Some hollies have leaves that taper to a point concavely (acuminate) or convexly

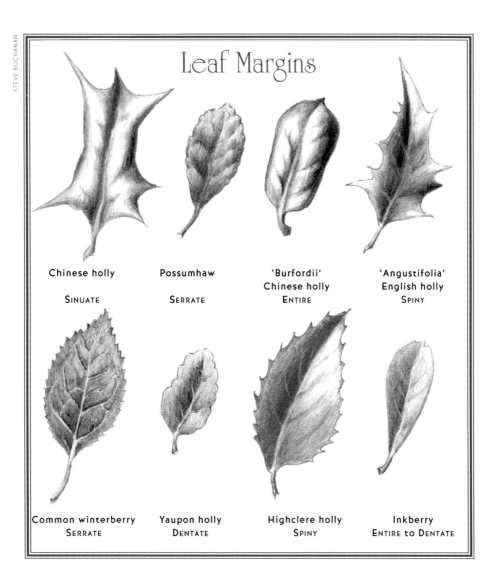

Leaf Margins

Chinese holly	**Possumhaw**	**'Burfordii'** **Chinese holly**	**'Angustifolia'** **English holly**
SINUATE	SERRATE	ENTIRE	SPINY

Common winterberry	**Yaupon holly**	**Highclere holly**	**Inkberry**
SERRATE	DENTATE	SPINY	ENTIRE to DENTATE

(acute). Others are abruptly pointed (apiculate), rounded and shallowly notched (retuse) or just plain rounded (obtuse). Some are spiny, some are not.

Leaf Base

The base of a holly leaf, where it attaches to the stalk, can be sharp (acute), blunt (obtuse), wedge-shaped (cuneate), rounded or nearly or quite straight (truncate).

Leaf Surface

The surface of a holly leaf, depending on the species, can be smooth (glabrous)

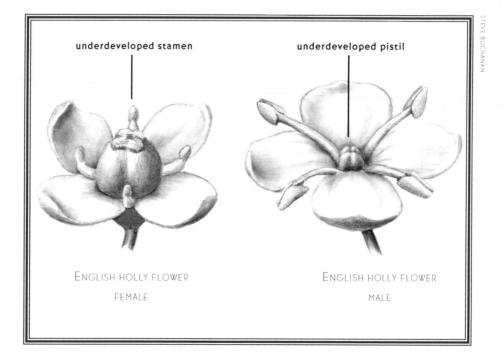

underdeveloped stamen   underdeveloped pistil

ENGLISH HOLLY FLOWER   ENGLISH HOLLY FLOWER

FEMALE   MALE

or hairy (hirsute) to varying degrees. Holly leaves run the gamut from dull to glossy.

The Sex Life of Hollies

Most people growing holly for the first time are surprised to learn that these plants generally are either male or female. Both sexes have flowers but only the females have berries. There must be a male plant with male flowers nearby to fertilize the female flowers if they are to produce viable fruit. (A few hollies, such as the English hollies, will bear fruit in the absence of a male plant. This process is called parthenocarpy. Parthenocarpic fruit has a tendency to drop before ripening. When it does persist and ripen, it is not viable and cannot germinate).

The pollen grains of holly are too heavy to become airborne. Pollination is usually accomplished by insects.

There are two ways to determine the sex of a holly plant. The first is to examine the flowers. Female flowers have underdeveloped stamens, lacking pollen; male flowers have underdeveloped pistils and do produce pollen. The second way is to observe whether or not a plant produces fruit. Fruit-producing plants are always female. Lack of fruit is not absolute proof of maleness, however, because unpollinated females also lack fruit.

• • •

Planting & Growing Hollies

BY ROBERT EMMERICH AND HERMAN C. GEHNRICH

Planting hollies is not much more difficult than planting other woody trees and shrubs. But there are a few rules you should follow to make sure your plant gets off to a good start.

Sun, Soil and Water

Selecting the right variety for your site is your first concern. Hollies are quite adaptable to the amount of sun available, but flowering, and therefore berrying, will generally be better on sites that receive some sun. Plants grown in shade will tend to be more open growing. American holly, *I. opaca,* is one species that will do quite well in light shade. Deciduous holly, however, shows a marked preference for sun, and berrying will be very sparse in shaded areas. Male plants, and even females that aren't expected to fruit heavily, can be grown very successfully as foliage plants in lightly shaded locations, and will provide excellent background and screening in the garden.

ROBERT EMMERICH, *an active member of the Holly Society of America and recipient of the Bronze Medal of the American Rhododendron Society, has grown hollies for more than forty years.*

HERMAN C. (BUD) GEHNRICH *is a member of the Board of Trustees of the Holly Society of America. He has received the Presidents Award of the HSA and the Bronze Medal of the ARS. Bud was largely responsible for the conception and realization of this handbook.*

When the roots of a container-grown plant are heavy and have circled the pot several times, cut vertically through the ball from one side to the other using a spade. Then pull the two halves apart, "butterflying" the root mass before planting.

Hollies are not particularly fussy about soils, but are partial to slightly acidic soils that are well drained and light in texture. A few hollies are quite tolerant of moisture: American holly will do well in very moist sites, providing it is not standing in water. Winterberry, *I. verticillata*, will usually be found in the wild growing in swamps (though usually in full sun); in the home garden it also succeeds in a well drained location, though it still needs sun if it is to fruit well.

The best times for planting are early spring and early fall — early spring, to get the plant established before the heat of summer, and early fall, so that the plant's roots become established before the onset of harsh winter weather.

No matter when you plant, watering is important throughout the first summer season. During hot weather, you'll need to water a recently planted holly, especially after a week when there has been less than an inch of rain.

Selecting the Plant

Inspect both burlapped and container-grown plants at the nursery to make sure there is no evidence of wilting or dried-out roots.

Examine the root system of container plants carefully to make certain that the plant has not become pot-bound. If it has, the roots will have circled around the inside of the pot and will be a solid, entangled mass. If the ball is planted as is, there is a good chance that the roots won't fan out into the soil and the plant will fail to develop properly. The ball must be disturbed and the roots cut to encourage them

to seek out the new soil. Where the roots are small, use a knife to cut the ball vertically in three or four places around the periphery, and then tease the roots out.

When the roots are heavy and have circled the pot several times, more drastic measures are in order. Using a spade, cut vertically through the ball from one side to the other. The cut should extend halfway up the ball from the bottom. Pull the two halves apart for planting, "butterflying" the root mass. Obviously, the best course of action is to buy plants that aren't so heavily root-bound.

Moving Established Plants

If you're planning to move an established holly, it's best to root prune it the season before moving. Insert a shovel or spade with a sharp, long blade into the ground all around the plant. A good rule of thumb is that the diameter of the root ball should be about as wide in feet as the diameter of the plant trunk is in inches. This root pruning should be done in late summer or very early fall. Remaining roots will send out fine new roots that will hold the soil and be able to take up moisture readily when the plant is moved. Because root growth continues until the ground gets quite cold, and starts again as soon as the ground begins to warm, the plant will be ready for moving by the following spring, although moving a year later would be all right as well.

If you plan to move an evergreen holly, the use of an antitranspirant is recommended. This product coats the leaves and reduces the amount of moisture lost to the atmosphere. The plant does not wilt as much after moving, and the coating gradually wears off. Sound irrigation practices should still be followed; the coating is not a substitute for watering.

In the past, it has been recommended that if you move a holly without root pruning it, you should top prune it to balance branch and leaf growth with the reduced root mass. Howev-

If you're planning to move an established holly, root prune it the season before moving. Insert a sharp shovel or spade into the ground all around the plant.

er, some recent research suggests that root-promoting auxins (growth hormones) are produced in buds at the ends of the branches and that transplanting without pruning is advisable. Until this difference of opinion is settled, it seems prudent to keep pruning after moving to a minimum. In any case, using an antitranspirtant is most important when the plant has not been root pruned. Water thoroughly before digging and moving the plant, preferably the day before so that moisture can move into all parts of the plant before any roots are cut.

Digging the Hole

Recommendations on planting trees and bushes have changed in recent years. Gardeners used to be admonished to dig a hole slightly wider and twice as deep as the root ball of the plant. Today, we are advised to put more effort into digging a wide hole, and making it only as deep as the root ball itself. The rationale for the new thinking is that this will prevent the plant from settling too deeply into the hole.

The hole should be at least twice as wide as the root ball. If the soil is of reasonably good quality, simply removing it from the ground and then replacing it

Dig a hole twice as wide and only as deep as the root ball, to prevent the plant from settling too deeply into the hole. If you're planting a burlapped plant, remove the burlap from at least the upper half of the root ball.

as fill after the holly has been put in place will suffice.

If you dig the hole too deeply and must put soil back in to raise it, make certain that the soil is well packed to prevent settling. As an alternative, place a flat rock under the ball to raise it. Since holly roots branch out and do not send out a tap root, the rock will not inhibit the growth of the plant.

If you're planting a burlapped plant, remove the burlap and twine from at least the upper half of the root ball. This is best done after the plant has been set in the planting hole, prior to backfilling, to minimize possible damage to the roots.

Another old practice of excessively amending the soil with peat moss, leaf mold, compost, manure and other materials is also frowned upon these days because it discourages the plant's roots from spreading out into the less inviting surrounding soil.

If the soil is poor and heavy and simply not suitable for hollies, you must amend the soil, but don't go overboard, and make sure the hole is large enough to provide adequate space for the root system to expand and support the tree.

Today, amendments such as compost, leaf mold and bark are preferred to the old standby, peat moss. Peat is difficult to soak thoroughly, and once it dries out, it will resist getting wet even when mixed in the soil. Also, peat is extracted from bogs. In addition, it is more expensive than many other suitable materials. In short, amend cautiously and select the right materials.

Don't fertilize at planting time; the tree should not be encouraged to send out new growth until it gets settled in.

Once it is planted, thoroughly water your holly and make sure that the fill is settled well into the hole — air spaces can be deadly to your new plant. Continue watering for several weeks, or more, depending on the weather.

IT TAKES TWO TO POLLINATE

If you have room for only one holly, select a female for the attractive berries. If no appropriate male hollies are nearby for pollination (within half a mile is usually close enough for bees to do the job), you'll need to purchase a male of the same species. If you don't have room, give it to a neighbor, who may wonder later why your plant has berries and his or hers doesn't.

Staking

Place stakes on opposite sides of tree-form hollies, being careful not to break through the root ball when you drive them into the ground. Don't tie the trunk too tightly to the stake; some motion should be possible. Tightly tied wire and even strong cord can girdle the trunk as the tree grows, cutting off the vital supply of water and nutrients to the top. Don't forget to remove the stakes and the tie when the tree has become established in a year or two, to prevent girdling. Also, remove any labels that might eventually girdle the plant.

Mulching

After planting, spread a two- to four-inch mulch over the root area, extending beyond the drip line of the plant. This conserves moisture in the soil and keeps the roots, which are near the surface of the soil, cool. Pine needles, leafmold, shredded bark and wood chips are all good natural mulches. Avoid black walnut chips, which contain a naturally occurring chemical that inhibits the growth of other plants.

A long-neglected holly may benefit from drastic pruning called "hat-racking." Cut back the holly until the top branches are short stubs. As you work downward, increase the length of the pruned branches to form a cone.

Don't rake up your leaves in autumn — they make a very satisfactory mulch, particularly if they're oaks. Maple leaves are less desirable as they tend to mat down and inhibit the exchange of air and moisture so important to the health of the tree. The idea is to approximate the conditions under which the plant grows in the wild, where there is a constant renewal of organic matter beneath the tree each year.

Pruning

Hollies will usually produce a well shaped specimen if given room to grow. Most of the spiny-leaved evergreen types tend to grow in a tall conical shape which can be maintained with a minimum of pruning. *I. opaca, aquifolium* and hybrids such as x *aquipernyi* will have a pleasing shape when young if they are pruned to a single leader and given an occasional judicious snip.

On the other hand, when some cultivars are ten or more years old, the neat habit disappears. Growth becomes more open and ragged, and new growth occurs near the ends of strong branches that grow upward. It's time for pruning to restore the shape and encourage new growth to fill in around the tree. This growth will sprout from the pruned branches because hollies have an abundance of latent buds under their bark.

For long-neglected hollies, a drastic pruning process called "hat-racking" may be worth a try. Cut back the holly until the top branches are short stubs. As you work downward, increase the length of the pruned branches to form a cone. The tree will be rather unsightly but should fill out nicely in a few years, forming many new shoots from the ends of the shortened branches. These should be thinned to remove the ones growing toward the center or straight up or down.

Several types of holly can be pruned into hedges and other decorative shapes. *I. crenata, I. cornuta* 'Dwarf Burford' and some of the blue hollies, such as 'Blue Girl' and 'Blue Boy', make outstanding evergreen hedges. Holly hedges can be sheared several times during the growing season to maintain their appearance. Some vigorous shoots may have to be removed occasionally. If so, cut them well below the outline of the hedge to eliminate stubs at the surface.

Pruning is best done during the dormant period. If you prune just before the holiday season you will have sprigs for decorations and wreaths, and your friends and neighbors will be delighted to accept your extra trimmings.

Long-term Maintenance

The amount of fertilizer needed by hollies will vary with the type of soil in your area. Nutrients filter quickly through light, sandy soils, while heavier soils, or those with a high organic content, will retain the fertilizer longer. Use one pound of fertilizer per inch of trunk diameter in light soils, less in richer soils. An all-purpose fertilizer such as 10-6-4 is a good choice and more economical than a specialized brand intended for broad-leafed evergreens.

As your holly matures, fertilize less so that the new growth is not so vigorous that it hides the fruit. A fertilizer high in phosphorus and potash is preferable for the older tree. The best time to fertilize is around the middle of March in the Middle Atlantic area. Avoid late summer and fall feeding so as not to stimulate late growth which might be winter killed. Spread the fertilizer evenly both inside and outside of the dripline of the tree but well away from the trunk.

In areas where hollies grow naturally there is usually enough rainfall to sustain growth. Once the holly is established, water only during droughts. During dry periods, soak the root area thoroughly once a week. This is much more beneficial than frequent shallow waterings.

• • •

Landscaping with Hollies

BY ROBERT ADAMS

At historic Williamsburg, Virginia, a tour guide recently led a group of visitors through the formal gardens of the Governor's Palace. One appreciative tour member extolled the exquisite quality of the "fine boxwood hedge" found throughout Williamsburg. The tour guide blushed slightly and replied, "Actually, most of the hedge is yaupon holly. We find it does much better than boxwood."

ROBERT ADAMS *gardens near Indianapolis, Indiana. Bob is a trustee of the Holly Society and the Magnolia Society, and a member of the International Plant Propagators Society.*

A row of weeping yaupon hollies softens a brick wall.

In the last 20 years, many gardeners have found that the genus *Ilex* provides superior plants for landscaping.

In recent years, more and more gardeners have discovered native and oriental deciduous hollies, which, with their bright fruits hanging picturesquely from their naked branches, provide more vibrant color in the winter landscape than the evergreen types. What's more, the fierce winters of the late 1970s brought on a search for new, hardier evergreen hollies, such as the blue hollies (*Ilex* x *meserveae*).

No holly testifies to these changes more than the native yaupon holly and its increased popularity in USDA hardiness zones 7b to 9 where it is hardy. Thanks largely to the efforts of a few nurseries such as the Tom Dodd Nursery in Alabama (and despite its unfortunate botanical name, *Ilex vomitoria*), several cultivars of this species are now available. There are dwarf, medium, tree form and weeping forms of yaupon holly. The berry color of this fine evergreen native ranges from red to yellow.

Designing with Hollies

Hollies are some of the most versatile of plants. Indeed, holly can satisfy the five basic garden design principles. First, holly can be used to suggest a path to lead you through the garden. Second, hollies can create an unsurpassed backdrop in the garden. The delicate colors of some magnolias, Chinese witch hazel, winter hazel and daphne are tastefully accented with an evergreen holly background. Third, hollies are an effective foil for other colors in the landscape. In their brilliant perennial borders, eminent British gardeners Gertrude Jekyll and William Robinson used strong elements such as a stone wall or an evergreen holly planting to stabilize the color scheme.

Hollies are also useful for creating a focal point in the garden and adding texture. No other plant genus succeeds so well in providing these elements in the landscape, from the tiny rock garden hollies to the majestic 80-foot hardy evergreen hollies, especially in the autumn and winter seasons. A fine example is the slope above the conservatory at Brookside Gardens in Wheaton, Maryland. Two great hollies dominate the crest of the hill with a deciduous forest in the background. One of the trees is the splendid American holly 'Dengle Belles' with orange and pinkish berries. The other holly is the lustrous *I.* x *attenuata* 'Sunny Foster' with leaves of varied golden hues on the sun-facing side of the tree.

Forms and Effects

Winter sun is hard on hollies that are tender in your area. Keep this in mind

A fruiting holly and a clematis-covered arbor announce the entrance to this garden.

This elegant cone-shaped American holly makes an outstanding specimen plant.

when choosing hollies, because one of the main attractions of evergreen varieties is the beautiful sheen reflected by that winter sun from the foliage and berries. Variegated hollies show well in shadier positions; they also tend to be less hardy than their solid green counterparts.

Over 90 percent of the hollies selected for good variegation are English hollies or their hybrids. John Wieman of Portland, Oregon, has devoted over fifty years to developing these hollies of fascinating color and leaf form. 'Betty Brite', 'Bright Bush' and 'Crinkle Green Variegated' are all variegated and dwarf in habit. His exquisite 'Moonlight' English holly cultivars can be used in containers or in the border to literally light up the landscape.

Most evergreen hollies demonstrate amazing resistance to pollution and salt spray. Landscapers often use both English and American hollies as screens and sound barriers along busy highways, or in hostile urban situations.

Deciduous hollies, native primarily to the eastern half of the United States, do well in Zones 4 through 9. Selections of *I. verticillata* by Robert Simpson of Vincennes, Indiana, and cultivars of *I. decidua* introduced by Bon Hartline of

Anna, Illinois, have created an insatiable demand among landscapers. The cross of the oriental *I. serrata* with *I. verticillata* produced such outstanding plants as 'Harvest Red', 'Sparkleberry' and 'Bonfire'.

Deciduous hollies prefer soils slightly acidic to neutral. They are much easier to grow than evergreen hollies because they require less nitrogen fertilizer, mulch and protection.

Now that gardeners have become enraptured by the native winterberry, *I. verticillata*, they are ready for the new cultivars of another eastern native, possumhaw, *I. decidua,* only recently available in the trade. Finches and mockingbirds adore this species, so grow at least one near your house for wintertime entertainment.

Yellow-berried cultivars of deciduous hollies tend to show better than reds in winter, especially when backed by a solid evergreen planting. *I. decidua* 'Byer's Golden' and 'Goldfinch' are hardy at least to USDA zone 5. *I. verticillata* 'Winter Gold' is a yellow-berried sport of the popular red-berried 'Winter Red'.

A most significant discovery in possumhaw culture was recently made by Clarence Hubbuch, horticulturist at Bernheim Forest in Clermont, Kentucky. Hubbuch found that *I. decidua* plants can easily be trained to single-stem standards, thereby creating stunning berried small trees with the plants' handsome gray bark exposed. Only minimal pruning of a few suckers is required for the first three to four years. Sprout inhibitors containing napthaleneacetic acid (NAA) make the task even easier.

The attractive bark patterns of holly impart a rugged beauty to the garden similar to that of the bark of mature beech trees. The bark of most species is a light-gray color. *I. serrata* and *I. verticillata* have black bark which contrasts well with their crimson-red berries.

Limbing up (that is, pruning the bottom branches of) beautiful hollies to show off their bark is a heart-rending procedure for some, but the result often will enrich the character of a winter garden. Limbing up a specimen or grove of small trees was a favorite design technique of the eminent landscape architect Thomas Church.

Keep in mind that hollies often need a good pruning every two or three years to retain good compact form, without errant branches here and there.

Both northern and southern gardeners have rediscovered an insect-resistant, carefree, hardy evergreen holly — the native inkberry, *I. glabra*. The lawn irrigation systems that cause yews to languish from overwatering make *I. glabra* thrive. Surprisingly, it also survives better than most hollies in neglected dry sites. The dwarf forms, such as 'Shamrock', make excellent semiformal, low-maintenance hedges.

For a generation now, southern landscapes have been planted with the great hybrid of English and Chinese hollies, *I.* x 'Nellie R. Stevens'. Many nurserymen now simply call it "Nellie." Nellie's popularity is being challenged by the new hybrids of lusterleaf holly, *I. latifolia,* with their six-inch, deeply veined, glossy leaves. These *I. latifolia* hybrids have an appeal comparable only to *Magnolia grandiflora.*

An early latifolia hybrid, 'Emily Bruner', is a cross with Chinese holly. The deep green gloss of its leaves and its heavy berries give an oriental effect. *I.* x 'Mary Nell' is a complex hybrid with a lighter green, deeply veined leaf. Nurserymen cannot satisfy the demand for these fine plants.

For gardens with limited space, dwarf or slow-growing hollies can fit the bill. Among the most attractive are two American hollies, 'Vera', an upright form, and 'Maryland Dwarf', a true dwarf and low spreading mound.

Japanese holly, *I. crenata,* and hybrids include many dwarf forms. 'Rock Garden' and 'Piccolo' are tiny one-foot-tall Japanese hollies that grow extremely slowly.

Fertilize dwarf cultivars sparingly to preserve their compact habits.

Hollies offer such a myriad of forms and effects in the landscape, you may want to check out one of the computer programs that have become available in the last few years to help design your garden. The best of these programs can truly help you make the transition from plant collector to landscape gardener. If you have an IBM compatible model, try Green Thumb Software, PO Box 18422, Boulder, CO 80308-8442; or MINDSUN (Gardenviews 5.1), Dept. H, RD 2, Box 710, Andover, NJ 07821. If you use an Apple computer, contact Terrace Software, PO Box 271, Medford, MA 02155.

Common winterberry and other deciduous hollies are stars in the winter garden.

• • •

Tips on Propagating Hollies

BY HAROLD L. ELMORE

M any holly growers don't even try to propagate hollies because they consider the process too complex, mysterious or difficult. The purpose of this chapter is to allay such concerns by describing the relatively simple principles underlying holly propagation, and to encourage holly enthusiasts to give it a try. There's nothing quite like the thrill of seeing tiny roots develop on the first cutting taken from one of your own hollies.

There are several ways to propagate holly: sprouting of seeds, severing of stolons (a form of division), layering, grafting, tissue culture and rooting of stem cuttings.

Almost all commercial and amateur propagators use the stem cutting process, which is the focus of this chapter. If you wish to explore some of the other propagation techniques listed above, consult *The Reference Manual of Woody Plant Propagation* by Michael A. Dirr and Charles W. Heuser Jr. (1987: Varsity Press, Athens, Georgia) or *Plant Propagation Practices* by James S. Wells (1985: American Nurseryman Publishing Co., Chicago, Illinois).

In the briefest terms, rooting of stem cuttings involves clipping a shoot from a growing holly, removing most of the leaves, wounding the base of the

HAROLD L. ELMORE *is the owner of Holly Haven Hybrids, a mail-order nursery in Knoxville, Tennessee, with a five-acre stock block of more than 600 different hollies. Hal has served Holly Society of America as President and Board Member, as well as in other capacities.*

Taking a cutting of American holly from the current season's growth.

cutting, treating it with a root-promoting chemical and sticking the prepared cutting into a damp rooting medium in a warm, humid, well lighted environment.

Choosing Cuttings

Although almost any branch of a holly can be encouraged to develop roots, you'll have better success if you select ideal cuttings at the ideal time. Cuttings should be from new growth of the current season (first year wood). If the shoot can be bent nearly 180 degrees without breaking, it is too immature. If it breaks with a snap, it is just right. Such cuttings are called "greenwood cuttings" and are best for most evergreen and some deciduous hollies.

Most deciduous holly cuttings should be taken earlier, at the "softwood cutting" stage, and then again in the fall, at the "hardwood cutting" stage.

The larger the diameter of the shoot the better, provided the wood is in the right condition.

Resist the temptation to select horizontal shoots so convenient to your pruning shears. Search instead for terminal and other shoots growing vertically. These will make much nicer plants.

Shoots closest to the roots of the mother plant will root best. Healthy, well fertilized and well watered plants produce the best cuttings.

When to Cut

Although seasons vary and the condition of new shoots ultimately determines when cuttings should be taken, an approximate calendar is helpful.

In hardiness zone 7, Chinese holly cuttings are often ready in July, as are cuttings of many of its interspecific hybrids. Japanese holly wood is ready in August, while September is better for English holly. Late fall or early winter is best for American holly.

These and other rooting parameters are summarized in "Propagation Guidelines," page 36.

How to Cut

Ideally, cuttings should be taken in the morning, while tissues are turgid (filled with water). Pruning shears are the usual tool for severing cuttings, though experienced propagators sometimes use a sharp knife.

Cuttings usually are 4 to 6 inches long, although much smaller and much larger cuttings can be used. Immediately protect cuttings from drying. Try to take all cuttings at approximately the same length.

Cuttings generally should be 4 to 6 inches long.

If preparing and sticking are to be delayed more than a few minutes, place the cuttings in an ice chest. Small numbers of cuttings can be preserved temporarily in a plastic bag containing a wet paper towel and placed in a refrigerator (not the freezer).

Preparing the Cuttings

Strip most of the leaves from each cutting, leaving 3 to 5 leaves at the upper end. Very large leaves can be cut in half (cleanly) to conserve space.

Use a sharp knife to "wound" each cutting by making a cut through the bark but not deep enough to enter the

Strip most of the leaves from each cutting, leaving 5 or so at the top.

woody part of the stem. Start about one inch (less on short cuttings) above the base and slice downward to the base, removing a narrow sliver of bark. This is called a "heavy wound," and is best for most hollies.

Roots will develop along the margins of these wounds. Larger-diameter cuttings can be wounded on both sides, resulting in a more balanced root system.

"Light wounds," thin vertical cuts made with knife tip or razor blade without removing any bark, work well with Japanese holly.

Hormone Treatment

Certain natural compounds can initiate and enhance rooting of stem cuttings. Though properly termed "auxins," these compounds are widely called "hormones." Practically all propagators use either indolebutyric acid (IBA) or napthaleneacetic acid (NAA), or a combination of both.

Some propagators prefer to prepare dilutions of the pure chemicals, but most take advantage of commercial preparations, either liquid or dry powder.

Commercial products commonly used include:

Hormodin #2	0.3% IBA powder	Merck & Co.
Hormodin #3	0.8% IBA powder	Merck & Co.
Hormo Root 2	2.0% IBA powder	Hortus Products Co.
Dip-N-Grow	1.5% IBA + NAA liquid	Alpkem Corp.

Both powder and liquid formulations have their strong adherents and detractors. Both methods work well on holly cuttings.

The cuttings should be immersed in liquid formulations from one second to 24 hours (the longer the contact, the greater the impact of the hormone); a 5-second dip is the most common practice.

The key to successfully rooting hollies is to match the condition of the cutting wood with the correct hormone treatment. If the treatment is too strong, the treated part of the cutting will blacken and the cutting will die; if too weak, the cutting will develop few if any roots.

The table "Propagation Guidelines" provides tips on when to cut and how much hormone to use for various species. All treatment concentrations listed in the table are achievable using the four commercial products listed above.

When experimenting with a new kind of holly, take cuttings during the first month shown in the table and use the weakest of the hormones indicated.

If all cuttings quickly blacken, remove and discard them. Wait two weeks and take another batch of cuttings and treat with the same hormone at the weakest concentration listed in the table.

On the other hand, if there is no sign of root development or even callus formation (white tissue at wound edges and/or cutting bases) after one month, re-treat the cuttings at a stronger concentration, or take a new batch of cuttings and use a stronger treatment.

Too many leaves have been stripped off of these cuttings.

Rooting Medium

Many different materials and mixtures have been used as the medium into which the holly cuttings are stuck. Coarse sand, peat-sand mixtures, perlite and peat-perlite mixtures are commonly used. My experience with many hollies is that a mixture of one part milled sphagnum peat moss to two parts horticultural perlite is close to ideal.

With a sharp knife, remove a sliver of bark at the base of the cutting.

There is a trend toward "direct sticking" — that is, the use of the same medium for rooting, usually in a small pot, and for growing on.

Prepare a well drained bed with the selected medium or fill individual small containers. Water the medium and let it drain several times to ensure saturation. Punch small holes in the medium to a depth of about one inch using a pencil, nail or anything having a diameter slightly larger than the cuttings. Insert treated cuttings into the holes just deeply enough to cover the hormone-treated area, and gently firm the medium around each cutting.

At this point the cuttings are under great physical stress and their survival depends on several rather heroic measures. The situation can be likened to that in a hospital when a patient goes into cardiac arrest — a monitor sounds an alarm, a nurse shouts "Code Blue!" and doctors and nurses come running.

Since the cuttings have been severed from their roots, the major source of water and nutrition has been cut off. Respiration continues in the leaves,

A PROPAGATION CHAMBER FOR BEGINNERS

If you want to root a few holly cuttings but are intimidated by all the gadgetry, consider a simple and inexpensive alternative — a propagation chamber that might also be called a miniature greenhouse or a portable coldframe. The basic structure is a standard polystyrene ice chest at least 12 inches tall.

- Use a sharp pencil to poke drainage holes every 6 to 8 inches through the bottom of the chest.
- Cut a piece of plastic window screen mesh to fit inside on the bottom of the chest to prevent plugging of the drain holes.
- Place one inch of pea gravel on top of the screen, followed by one inch of coarse sand.
- Add 3 inches of damp peat-perlite rooting medium. Sprinkle several times to moisten thoroughly and allow to drain overnight.
- Stick cuttings as described earlier.
- Moisten the top edge of the ice chest and cover the entire top of the chest with very thin (about 1/2 mil) polyethylene, the type used by many dry-cleaners. This thin plastic allows essential exchange of carbon dioxide and oxygen while preventing the escape of water vapor.

but dehydration begins to inhibit cell function. The cuttings are minutes from death.

However, if leaves are kept coated with thin sheets of water, rehydration occurs. Also, cool temperatures will minimize respiration, stabilizing the cuttings' vital processes so that they can survive for several hours or even several days.

Then, if leaves are exposed to enough light, photosynthesis will replace the energy lost through respiration. Once these critical needs are met, cuttings can be tucked into a warm, well lighted bed of friendly medium where photosynthe-

---

- Place your completed propagation unit where air temperature averages 70 degrees F and where additional light, as much as practically possible, can be provided.

- Note: do not expose the unit to direct sunlight; this can cause inside temperature to shoot up in excess of 100 degrees F (38 degrees C) and cook the cuttings.

- Resist the temptation to examine cuttings during the first week.

  Whenever you open the unit, sprinkle the cuttings lightly before carefully reinstalling the polyethelene sheet. Otherwise, watering is not necessary.

- For your first trial, use Chinese or Japanese holly or the hybrid cultivars 'Mary Nell' and 'Nellie R. Stevens', all of which are relatively easy to root. If all goes well, you should see roots on at least half of your cuttings in a month.

- After cuttings are well rooted, lift gently and pot into individual pots under ample light.

- In summer, cuttings can go outside in nursery beds in partial shade for several years before taking their places in the landscape.

- Keep fall- and winter-rooted cuttings indoors until after frost danger the following spring.

PROPAGATION GUIDELINES

ILEX SPECIES	ROOTING SEASON[1]	HORMONE CONCENTRATION[2]
aquifolium	Sept. to Feb.	0.8%T to 2.0%T
cassine	Sept. to Feb.	0.8%T to 2.0%T
cornuta	July to March	0.3%T to 0.8%T
crenata	Aug. to Feb.	0.3%T to 0.8%T
decidua	June or Oct.	10%Q or 0.8%T
glabra	Sept. to March	0.3%T to 0.8%T
opaca	Oct. to March	0.8%T to 2.0%T
pedunculosa	Oct. to Feb.	0.8%T
pernyi	Sept. to Dec.	0.8%T
serrata	June or Oct.	10%Q or 0.8%T
verticillata	June or Oct.	10%Q or 0.8%T
x *altaclerensis*	Aug. to Oct.	0.8%T to 2.0%T
x *aquipernyi*	Aug.	0.8%T
x *attenuata*	Oct. to March	0.8%T to 2.0%T
x *koehneana*	Sept. to March	0.8%T to 0.8%Q
x *meserveae*	Aug. to March	0.3%T to 0.8%T

[1] Schedule is for hardiness zone 7. Colder zones: later for spring/summer cuttings; earlier for fall/winter. Warmer zones: earlier for spring/summer cuttings; later for fall/winter.

[2] First concentration shown applies to the earlier date; second to the later date. T equals indolebutyric acid (IBA) in talc, Q equals liquid 5 second quick dip (10% Dip-N-Grow v/v).

sis will replace energy lost through respiration, and cuttings have the opportunity to complete their recovery by replacing missing roots at their leisure.

The cuttings have been dipped in rooting powder.

Humidity

Virtually 100 percent relative humidity in the air surrounding the cuttings will assure complete rehydration. Most professional propagators use an intermittent mist system. Although misting systems are useful, they're relatively complex, fairly expensive and subject to mechanical failure. One less complex alternative is a cold frame, usually sunken into the ground. If kept tightly closed, humidity in excess of 90 percent can be attained in a cold frame. Cold frames have been used for centuries and are preferred by some propagators even today.

Six weeks later, a healthy root ball has formed.

Bottom Heat

Little if any rooting takes place below 55 degrees F; 70 to 75 degrees F is ideal. This means that propagation may be undertaken in summer months without much attention to the temperature of the rooting medium.

However, since many holly species root best during fall and winter, you'll have to arrange to warm the medium. Techniques include hot water carried through metal or plastic pipes, hot air directed up through the medium and various electrical heating systems using wire grids or mats. Consult Lloyd C. Hahn's "A Dirt Farmer's Method of Rooting Holly," *Holly Society Journal*, Vol. 4, No. 4, Autumn 1986 for a detailed description of a system useful for a small scale operation.

The ongoing respiration in the leaves of holly cuttings can be balanced out by photosynthesis if leaves are exposed to about 100 foot-candles of light. If more intense light can be provided, cuttings can develop into more vigorous plants.

Of course, additional light often means more heat, which means more moisture must be applied to the leaves to maintain the high humidity necessary for rooting.

Special artificial grow lights are widely used in propagation. However, many propagators find that ordinary fluorescent lamps are quite adequate — and less expensive.

Remember that light intensity diminishes with the square of the distance from a source. Intensity at one foot away from a lamp is 4 times greater than at 2 feet, 9 times greater than at 3 feet, and 16 times greater than at 4 feet. In short, a light source is more efficient if close to the cuttings.

Preventing Diseases

The optimum conditions for rooting cuttings are also ideal for many plant disease organisms. It's important to keep work surfaces sterile. However, you can often avoid disease problems simply by mixing fresh peat-perlite rooting medium for each batch of cuttings, and discarding the old medium after one use (it is a good amendment for garden soil). Perlite is essentially sterile, and fresh peat moss is mildly fungicidal.

PROPAGATION EQUIPMENT AND SUPPLIES

Brighton By-Products Co.
P.O. Box 23
New Brighton, PA 15066
Catalog, $5

Florist Products
2242 North Palmer Dr.
Schaumburg, IL 60173
Free catalog

E.C. Geiger
P.O. Box 285, Rt. 63
Harleysville, PA 19438
Free catalog

Mellingers, Inc.
2310 West South Range Rd.
North Lima, OH 44452
Free catalog

• • •

What's Eating Your Hollies?

BY AL COOK

Compared to such pest-of-the-month plants such as willows, plums, cherries and honey locust, hollies are subject to comparatively few serious insect pests. The worst offenders vary by region and sometimes even within a particular locale.

For most of us in the Midwest, the primary offenders are leaf miners, which devastate the leaves of our American holly (*Ilex opaca*), and spider mites, which suck our once-green Japanese holly (*I. crenata*) to deathlike gray. Not many other crawlies bother hollies in the Midwest, except black vine weevil in landscapes lacking sufficient *Taxus* and *Euonymus* species to satiate them.

In the Northwest, relatives of the leaf miner pests of American holly do similar ugly work and ruin the glossy leaves of English holly *(I. aquifolium)*. Holly bud moths also bother English hollies in the Northwest, feeding and making webs on new growth. Lesser nuisances (unless they're in your own yard) include leaf rollers, scales, mites and aphids.

From the East Coast, we hear wailings about hollyberry midge, the wormy stages of which ruin the red fruits of American holly, rendering them forever green and noncontrasty with the foliage come yuletide. What good are green holly berries?

Only other holly fanatics can appreciate the enormity of such a calamity.

Holly folks in the East also suffer from leaf miners, and mites of various persuasions, and a half-dozen or so species of scale insects, nasty little sap suckers that build various protective coverings over themselves. (Lest we pass lightly or blithely past scale insects, let us ponder that some 70 percent of the insects that

Southern red mites suck vital juices from holly leaves. Horticultural soaps and oils can keep mite populations in bounds.

regularly violate hollies are scale insect species.) In some areas of the East, a real gaggle of holly-hurting insects and such (in addition to midges, miners, mites and scales) are tallied: aphids, mealybugs, whiteflies, budmoth, miscellaneous beetles and weevils and even grasshoppers.

To complicate matters, the East is a complex region, geologically and climatologically. Thus one side of a hill may have one bug, the valley below may be plagued by another pest and the far side of the hill may be clean.

Reports from the South are similar to those of the East.

Pest Control, General

Good culture is a great preventive tactic. Everyone knows that healthy plants will ward off predators (everyone except a given predator, that is). Give hollies room to enjoy their own patches of air. Give them loamy soil, well aerated and well drained. Give generously of mulch and decently of fertilizer, and water deeply once a week or so during droughts.

Selection of resistant species and cultivars is another good ploy. A quick scan of the literature reveals that American and English hollies can be soup kitchens for a variety of insects and mites. Other evergreen species and hybrids

Berries infested by the hollyberry midge are smaller and don't turn uniformly red.
Handpick and destroy infected fruits.

(especially blue hollies, *I. meserveae*) are usually slightly immune to six- and eight-legged predators. Check with local authorities for cultivars resistant to mite species common to your area.

Some cultivars of American holly seem less susceptible to hollyberry midge than others — notably 'Miss Helen' and 'Vera'. Some Japanese holly cultivars shamelessly entice mites, while others, such as *I. crenata*, are much more resistent to mites.

If robust health and/or the choice of a resistant species or cultivar fail to keep insects and other small creatures away, the next step is to indentify the predators. Check bookstores and libraries for relevant books. Botanic gardens and arboretums can help, as can your Cooperative Extension office.

Maybe the things you see crawling over your hollies are innocent, just passing by. Maybe they are good guys, looking for the real holly pests to devour.

When it is obvious that the things really are deleterious to holly, it's time to meditate for a while, seeking revelations as to the population density you can live with. Surely one splotchy leaf is not cause for kamikase tactics. Maybe mites will diminish after the rain that meteorologists are predicting. Or maybe you are compelled to do something to save your holly's looks or life. Then and only then,

Tea scale on a Chinese holly. Scale can be controlled with horticultural oils, especially when they are in their crawling stages.

go for the bombs. Some weapons, of course, are less dangerous than others.

Look for "environmentally friendly" methods:

Horticultural soaps and oils will get some insects, mites and other pests, and seldom harm children or pets. Regular sprays of just plain water, somewhat forceful but not to the point of dislodging plant parts, have chalked up impressive statistics in the bug game. These sprays must hit the undersides of leaves for good results.

Handpicking is truly a nontoxic technique. This method is too tedious for most insect problems but is useful for hollyberry midge.

As a last resort, consider legal pesticides and/or miticides. Determine which materials are legal and effective. Consult your Cooperative Extension agent for advice on the most up-to-date pesticides to use. Fellow holly maniacs may offer advice, but some may be ignoring the book when they recommend plutonium, say, for leaf rollers. It is best to be safe, sure and legal.

Use chemicals (including soaps and oils) according to manufacturers' and lawmakers' recommendations and restrictions. Also, use a modicum of common sense. Never spray into the wind. Wash up after each chemical warfare sortie. Never mix more than you can use at one time. Triple rinse empty pesticide containers and sprayers. Check local regulations for disposal of empty containers.

Leaf miners have left their mark on this holly. Call your Cooperative Extension agent for the latest recommendations.

Pests and Controls

Leaf Miners

Leaf miner insects begin as flies that punch holes in leaves of some holly species (mostly *I. opaca, I. aquifolium* and *I. vomitoria*) and lay eggs therein. Eggs hatch into clever little larvae that eat the innards out of holly leaves, leaving ugly brown irregular tunnels that turn brown. Adult flies, when flying around before laying eggs, can be hit with various legal contact insecticides.

After eggs are laid and hatched, larvae think they are safe between the upper and lower leaf skins, but a systemic pesticide (one that penetrates plant tissue) can fool them.

Mites

Mites and their ilk are somewhere between pinhead and pinpoint in size. They revel in hot, dry weather, proliferating prodigiously on the undersides of holly leaves, sucking vital juices. Infested leaves go off-color, whitening, graying or browning, and masses of delicate webbing develops. The so-called "false spider mites" look like true mites and cause similar damage but produce no webs.

Sprays of horticultural soaps and oils are effective. As an alternative, you can try regular sprays of plain water as mentioned above.

Scale Insects

Scale insects in feeding stages are usually little convex things on stems and/or leaves. They range in size from about the width of a soft-pencil mark to fingernail size. Shapes are round or oval or blobby. Colors are varied. Some scale insects look like tiny eyes, or fried eggs. Some are hard, some rubbery, some squishy.

Not only do scale insects suck plant juices, causing damage to infested plant parts and even death, but some also excrete stuff politely termed "honey dew," which gives rise to sooty mold which does no harm to hollies but often worries the bejabbers of holly owners.

Armored scale insects (with hard coverings that more or less protect them from chemicals) can be reduced in numbers with horticultural oils. Other scale species may be controlled with oil or other legal pesticides, especially during the crawling stages when the little rascals are out from under their rooflike covers.

Hollyberry Midge

Of the big hitters among holly predators, hollyberry midge is the hardest to control. Adults fly around about the time that American hollies flower and lay eggs in the flower ovules. If you kill them at this time you'll probably also kill the bees that pollinate the flowers. Thus no pretty berries. And yet, after fruits begin to form, the midge maggots are safely inside. The infected fruits will be smaller than normal. Worst of all, they'll lack some or all of the dramatic color for which they're famous.

So far, handpicking and destroying affected fruits is the only way to go.

Black Vine Weevil

Black vine weevil is a reclusive sort of vandal. Grubs chew merrily on roots, out of sight in the soil. Adults creep out of the ground at night and chew characteristic semicircular notches in the margins of leaves. Recommended retaliation involves applying pesticides thoroughly to foliage during late spring and summer.

A Final Note

There's a reason why no specific insecticides, other than soap and oil, are mentioned above. There's a very good chance that a chemical pesticide legal today won't be legal tomorrow. Call your local Cooperative Extension agent for the latest recommendations.

• • •

An Introduction to Diseases of Holly

BY J.L. PETERSON

T he *Index of Plant Diseases in the United States* lists an impressive 65 different genera of fungi on holly. Many of them include more than one species, increasing this number considerably. Holly may also be affected by bacteria, nematodes and viruses. Considering the number of organisms reported as parasitizing holly, it's a wonder that this plant manages to survive in nature at all!

Fortunately, most of these organisms are not aggressive on holly and holly diseases are generally not serious. This isn't to say that holly diseases are never a problem, as some diseases can be quite serious when the right environmental conditions are present.

Plant diseases and their causes are classified as abiotic or biotic. Abiotic diseases are usually the result of unfavorable environmental conditions. These are also known as nonpathogenic or noninfectious diseases. Such factors as winter injury, drought, excess moisture, unbalanced nutrition, genetic plant weaknesses and mechanical damage fall in this category.

Biotic diseases, which are also called pathogenic or infectious, are caused by living organisms. A large number of the organisms reported on holly are considered secondary or weakly pathogenic; in other words, they live on weakened or dead portions of the plant. Some of these organisms do not penetrate the plant directly, but rather enter following damage from

DR. J. L. PETERSON *is retired from the Department of Plant Pathology, New Jersey Agricultural Experiment Station, Rutgers University, New Brunswick, New Jersey.*

more aggressive parasites or through the wounds of a mechanically injured plant.

Diagnosing Diseases

To diagnose a plant disease you must know the symptoms of the disease. Then you must look for signs of the cause of the disease and patterns of occurrence.

The following steps are helpful in diagnosing a disease:

1. Determine what part of the plant is actually affected. Damage on the southwest side may indicate winter injury. Death of or damage on older leaves only may indicate a pathogenic disease or damage from chemical pesticides. Dead branches scattered throughout a plant may indicate cankers. If the whole plant is discolored or dying, a root disease, nutritional disorder, drought or excess moisture may be involved.

2. Observe the pattern of disease occurrence, particularly in larger plantings. Is the problem associated with a particular terrain? Are some areas free from the disease? How do these areas differ?

3. Look for differences in susceptibility among holly varieties. Are some cultivars affected less than others?

4. Look for mechanical damage to trunk or roots. Such things as bark splitting or peeling, animal damage and recent excavations near the root zone may be important.

5. Look for signs of fungus, such as fruiting bodies, on the plant. Keep in mind that some fungus problems on hollies are caused by only part of the life cycle of the particular fungus. A fungus may spend another part of its life cycle on dead organic matter such as leaves, an alternate host plant of another species or even in association with an insect. Does the organism, if present, seem to be following the damage, or did it cause the problem in the first place? Note if insects or other parasites are present. Generally, insects are more damaging to holly than diseases.

6. If you don't find anything above ground that indicates the cause of the problem, examine the roots, specifically root coloring and areas of most active growth. Is the entire plant affected, or only the upper portion?

7. Determine if the problem is recent or has been there for some time, causing a steady decline. Does the problem become more serious at certain times of the year?

8. Note which cultural practices have been used, such as fertilization or use of an herbicide.

COMMON DISEASE SYMPTOMS

🌿 **LEAF SPOTS.** Tar spots, caused by the fungus *Phacidium*, are one of the more common leaf-spot diseases. Yellow spots appear on the leaves early in summer and generally turn reddish brown as the season progresses. By fall, small, tarlike spots appear in discolored areas. Avoiding plant crowding and pruning to improve air circulation in the lower branches will help.

🌿 **CANKERS AND DIE-BACK.** Cankers are characterized by sunken, cracked areas on stems or limbs. The various species of fungi that generally cause them usually enter through wounds in the bark. Twig and branch die-back, usually associated with cankers, may also be caused by these fungi. Removal of the affected limbs by pruning well below the canker area will help control these diseases.

🌿 **GRAY MOLD.** During prolonged moist weather the fungus *Botrytis* can cause a blossom blight of holly. In severe cases, the fungus will spread to adjacent leaves and twigs, causing a die-back.

🌿 **WOOD ROT.** Large, conspicuous fungi often appear on dead or dying holly branches. These are secondary fungi which rot wood previously killed by some other cause. Where possible, prune out the dead wood of the affected holly.

🌿 **SOOTY MOLD.** A superficial black sootlike covering on the upper surfaces of leaves is caused by *Fumago* and other species of fungi. The unsightly leaf covering can be easily rubbed off the leaf. The leaf is not directly damaged, as the fungi live on insect droppings or "honeydew" covering the leaf surface, although leaves may tend to yellow beneath the heavy sooty coverings.

🌿 **LEAF-DROP AND BROWNING.** Holly leaves often turn yellow or brown and fall. This simply may be natural leaf drop, or it may be caused by severe drought or winter injury. If the drought occurs in summer, leaf-drop may be particularly noticeable the following spring. During cold windy winters, unprotected holly may lose leaves and branches fail to leaf out the following year. Select cultivars with proven hardiness in your area.

Once you've determined the cause, you can choose the proper control measures. There are two types of disease control: cultural and chemical. Cultural control involves changing the plant's environment so that it is more favorable for plant growth and less favorable for the disease.

Don't just reach for the pesticide. In general, prevention is the best control. Some infectious diseases can be prevented by using a resistant holly cultivar, or by changing the growing conditions of a susceptible holly. Prevention may also involve reducing the source of infection by pruning out dead plant parts, cleaning up infected leaves and twigs from the soil surface and wholesale removal of dead plants.

If the disease is caused by an environmental or abiotic factor, or if a biotic disease is of secondary nature following stress of the plant, generally it will do little good to apply a pesticide. And applying pesticides after the symptoms are noticeable may not be the time the organism is most vulnerable to the treatment.

If you must resort to the use of a chemical, be aware that government regulations change constantly. Your local Cooperative Extension Service is the best place to go for the most up-to-date pesticide recommendations.

Further Reading

For information on identifying specific holly diseases, consult:

Farr, D.F., et al. 1989. *Fungi on Plants and Plant Products in the United States.* APS Press. St. Paul, Minnesota.

Guba, E.F. and J.D. Stevenson, 1963. "Fungus and Nematode Inhabitants of Holly (*Ilex*)." *AES Bul. 530*, University of Massachusetts.

Pirone, P.P., 1978. *Diseases and Pests of Ornamental Plants 5th ed.* J. Wiley and Sons, New York.

U.S. Dept. of Agri. 1980 Agri. Handbook 165. *Index of Plant Diseases in the United States.* U.S. Govt. Printing Office.

Reprinted and adapted from *Diseases of Holly in the United States, Bulletin No. 19*, Holly Society of America, 1982 (out of print). The balance of the 44-page booklet covers biotic and abiotic diseases in detail.

HOLLIES
for the
Home Garden

American Holly
Ilex opaca

Ilex opaca **'Satyr Hill'**

Eastern United States   **5 to 9**

OUTSTANDING FEATURES:

Hardiness is a cardinal attribute of this evergreen holly species, which can grow to 50 feet tall or more. Leaves are dark green, usually not glossy. Abundant small berrylike fruits (2/5 inch in diameter) come in all shades of red and orange; yellow on some cultivars.

HABIT AND USE:

Conical when young; open and rounded small tree when mature. Popular for specimens and tall hedges. An important source of midwinter food for birds.

HOW TO GROW:

Give this species loamy, well drained, slightly acidic soil, organic mulch beneath branches, nitrogen fertilizer every season and sunny or partly shady exposure. Avoid-windy locations. Regular selective pruning (not shearing) will maintain compact but natural looking form. Leafminer, holly berry midge and scale can be a problem, depending on the region.

VARIETIES AND RELATED SPECIES:

Many cultivars. Some of the better ones are:

'Canary' — A good yellow-fruited selection.

'Farage' — A fine conical shape with superior red fruits, popular from Indiana to Long Island.

'Hedgeholly' — Not restricted to hedges as name implies. A dense compact grower, usually as broad at base as it is tall. Good red fruit display.

'Jersey Knight' — An excellent male for pollinating.

'Jersey Princess' — Hardier than some. Leaves glossier than most. Vivid red fruits.

'Lacquerberry' — Very large glossy red fruits.

'Miss Helen' — One of the most adaptable and dependable red-fruited clones, performs well in Midwest, East and upper South.

'Old Heavy Berry' — An old favorite, sturdy in appearance. Large, dark lustrous leaves and red fruits.

'Villanova' — Large golden-yellow fruits.

Aquipern Holly
Ilex x *aquipernyi*

Ilex x *aquipernyi* **'Gable's Male'**

Hybrid

6b to 9

PARENTAGE:

aquifolium x *pernyi*

OUTSTANDING FEATURES:

Small, spiny evergreen leaves; fruits are dark red, rarely yellow.

HABIT AND USE:

Large shrubs or small cone-shaped trees excellent for specimens, corners of large buildings, screens and hedges

HOW TO GROW:

Same as English Holly.

VARIETIES AND RELATED SPECIES:

'San Jose' — A favorite in the Southwest. 20 foot conical shape covered with large dark red fruit. (Don't confuse with an *I.* x *koehneana* cultivar also called 'San Jose'.

'Rock Garden' — A tiny evergreen plant only a foot to 18 inches high and twice as wide. Excellent in small gardens or as bonsai.

'September Gem' — A large evergreen shrub with an early display of bright red fruits persisting into winter.

Ilex 'September Gem'

PAMELA HARPER

Blue Holly (Meserve Holly)
Ilex x *meserveae*

Ilex x *meserveae* **'Blue Princess'**

Hybrid

5b to 9a

PARENTAGE:

rugosa x *aquifolium*

OUTSTANDING FEATURES:

Medium-sized, bushy cold-hardy selections. Bluish purple stems and lustrous blue-green, spiny, evergreen foliage, somewhat finer in texture than most Chinese and American types, usually with shining red fruits. The blue hollies are famous for eye appeal and history: an amateur gardener, Mrs. F. Leighton (Kathleen) Meserve, made the pollen transfer that originated this family of marvelous holly cultivars.

HABIT AND USE:

Mostly rounded and compact, blue hollies are used in foundation plantings, hedges (sheared or lightly trimmed or seldom touched), and mass plantings. In Zones 5 and 6a, most cultivars will not attain the sizes typical in milder areas. For example, 'Blue Princess' readily grows to 8 feet or more in Zone 7; specimens taller than 5 feet tall are unusual in Zone 5b.

HOW TO GROW:

In northern limits of hardiness, it is wise to use organic mulch, provide protection from winter wind, irrigate during dry times and apply fertilizer annually. These hollies respond well to careful pruning for neatness, but shearing imparts unnatural stiffness. In warmer zones, partial shade during summer afternoons is helpful, as well as mulch.

VARIETIES AND RELATED SPECIES:

'Blue Princess' — A dependable heavy-fruiting cultivar with glossy spiny leaves and rounded compact form.

'Blue Prince' — A popular male cultivar for pollen. Taller and a tad hardier than 'Blue Princess', this selection is a valuable landscape plant even though it is fruitless.

'Blue Maid' — A good fruiting female and a faster grower than 'Blue Princess' (some say it is also hardier but others disagree).

'Blue Angel' — A female with purple stems and good red fruits, this is the slowest growing blue holly cultivar but unfortunately is the least hardy (grows fine in Zone 7).

'Blue Stallion' — A vigorous robust male with dark green foliage without sharp spines.

An excellent pollinator because of long blooming season. A great foliage plant for evergreen screening.

'Golden Girl' — A yellow-fruited cultivar. Sometimes erroneously called blue hollies, but actually from different parentage (*cornuta* x *rugosa*), are two excellent cultivars. They are hardier than the blues and more tolerant of hot weather, but their foliage is lighter green and not as glossy. Untrimmed, they mature at about 10 feet tall and equally wide.

'China Girl' — Plenty of large, 1/3-inch red fruits on a compact shrub.

'China Boy' — Male companion to ensure fruiting of the female above.

EVERGREEN

Chinese Holly
Ilex cornuta

Ilex cornuta **'O' Spring'**

Eastern China and Korea   **7 to 9**

OUTSTANDING FEATURES:

Large, dark, shiny green leaves, sometimes to 4 inches long, often strongly rectangular, usually with sharp spines. Prolific red fruits (1/4 to 1/2 inch across) set without pollination (a male plant is not needed) and hang on till spring.

HABIT AND USE:

Compact growth. Various cultivars are useful for foundation and corner planting, screens and impenetrable hedges.

HOW TO GROW:

Chinese hollies are adaptable to slightly alkaline as well as acidic soils, and they are quite drought tolerant. They fruit most heavily in full sun. See English Holly. Watch for scale insects.

VARIETIES AND RELATED SPECIES:

The species is widely used in zones 7 and 8; popular cultivars include:

'Berries Jubilee' — Abundant, very large red fruits are set off by large spiny foliage. Compact growth to 6 to 8 feet in time.

'Burfordii' — A popular cultivar, will become a massive shrub or small tree, often too large for small gardens. Abundant large red fruit.

'Dwarf Burford' — Sometimes incorrectly called 'Burfordii Nana', similar to 'Burfordii' except that it is slower-growing by about half and has smaller leaves and fruits.

'O' Spring' — Handsome leaves variegated with light green, yellow and cream in irregular patterns. Male.

'Rotunda' — Another "people-stopper" with very spiny leaves. Compact growth, 6 feet tall in time. Red fruits on older plants.

Some notable hybrid cultivars:

'Emily Bruner' — (*cornuta* 'Burfordii' x *latifolia*). Zone 6b to 9. A large, 20-foot evergreen shrub with large leaves (to 4 inches long) and good red fruit.

'James Swan' — (*cornuta* 'Burfordii' x *latifolia*). Zone 6b to 9. A handsome male pollinator for 'Emily Bruner'.

'Doctor Kassab' — (*cornuta* x *pernyi*). Zone 6b to 9. A compact, narrowly conical to columnar form to 20 feet tall. Glossy evergreen foliage, excellent red fruits.

'Lydia Morris' — (*cornuta* x *pernyi*). Zone 6b to 9. Densely conical, large shrub with handsome spiny foliage and red fruits. About 12 feet tall and wide at maturity.

'John T. Morris' — The pollinating male selection for 'Lydia Morris' and others.

'Mary Nell' — ([*cornuta* x *pernyi* 'Red Delight'] x *latifolia*). Zone 7 to 9, extremely glossy, broadly lanceolate evergreen leaves. Rich red fruits. A superior holly.

'Nellie R. Stevens' — (*cornuta* x *aquifolium*). Zone 6b to 9. A highly popular evergreen in the South. Conical shape to 20 feet tall. Lustrous leaves with few spines. Good Chinese-red fruit. A real winner.

PATRICIA JOSEPH

Dahoon Holly
Ilex cassine

Yellow-berried cultivar

Southeastern United States   **8 to 9a**

OUTSTANDING FEATURES:

A fine small evergreen tree, 20 to 25 feet tall. Produces a profusion of small brightly colored fruits (usually red) that persist.

HABIT AND USE:

This semirounded densely branched small tree is useful as an accent plant or patio tree and in group plantings.

HOW TO GROW:

A tolerant species, adaptable to most soils, including wet acidic conditions. Mulch, prune occasionally and fertilize annually.

VARIETIES AND RELATED SPECIES:

'Baldwin' — Red fruits, upright conical habit.

'Lowei' — Yellow fruits.

var. *myrtifolia* — Tiny, narrow, willow-like leaves.

PAMELA HARPER

English Holly
Ilex aquifolium

Ilex aquifolium **'Angustifolium'**

England, Europe, western Asia,   **6 to 8b**
northern Africa

OUTSTANDING FEATURES:

Evergreen foliage is superb, featuring richly glossy leathery leaves, typically wavy edged, with sharp spines on leaf margins and tips. Leaves of some selections are variegated with silvery white or bright yellow. Small white fragrant flowers and subsequent bright red (yellow on some cultivars) 1/4-inch or larger fruits are borne on previous year's growth. Mature size varies from 20 to 40 feet tall, from wide to narrow.

HABIT AND USE:

Typical form is broadly conical when young, becoming round-topped at maturity, with dense foliage usually to the ground. Useful for screens, hedges and specimens, and cut sprays of berries and foliage are prized for holiday decorating.

HOW TO GROW:

Grows best in rich, well drained soil and a humid moderately cold climate (such as the Pacific Northwest and the Atlantic Coast from Massachusetts to Chesapeake Bay). Full sun is needed for maximum berry production, but afternoon shade and ample water is necessary in hot dry climates. This species responds well to pruning, even shearing. Annual fertilization, especially nitrogen, helps ensure good glossy foliage. Also benefits from a 3-inch layer of organic mulch such as wood chips or shredded bark.

VARIETIES AND RELATED SPECIES:

There are endless variations in foliage size and color, fruit color and growth habit, but those available in the nursery trade are limited.

'Angustifolia' — Available as either male and female, slow growing with small, narrow leaves. A good choice for limited space.

'Balkans' — Somewhat more cold hardy than most English hollies. Available in either sex.

'Sparkler' — Bears large clusters of red fruits at an early age.

'Argentea-marginata' — This is not a single cultivar, but rather a group of female types with silver-edged leaves, including 'Silvery', 'Silver Queen' and 'Silver Edge'.

EVERGREEN

Highclere Holly
Ilex x *altaclerensis*

Ilex x *altaclerensis* **'Camelliaefolia'**

NATIVE HABITAT:	HARDINESS ZONE:
Hybrid	**7 to 9, 6b in protected spots**

PARENTAGE:

aquifolium x *perado*

OUTSTANDING FEATURES:

Handsome evergreen leaves, often large and sometimes spineless. Red fruits. Often confused with English holly.

HABIT AND USE:

Vigorous large shrubs or small trees, good specimen plants, useful for screen plantings.

HOW TO GROW:

Easy to grow where cold hardy, somewhat tolerant of air pollution and salt spray. Organic mulch over root zone and annual fertilization are advisable. Prune as needed to keep appearance tidy.

VARIETIES AND RELATED SPECIES:

'Camelliaefolia' — Large lustrous leaves 5 inches long. New shoots are purple, abundant fruits are dark red.

'James G. Esson' — A vigorous female, deep green, with profuse red fruits.

'T. H. Everett' — A reliable male for pollinating.

'Wilsonii' — An old favorite female with vigorous compact conical habit and prolific vivid red fruits.

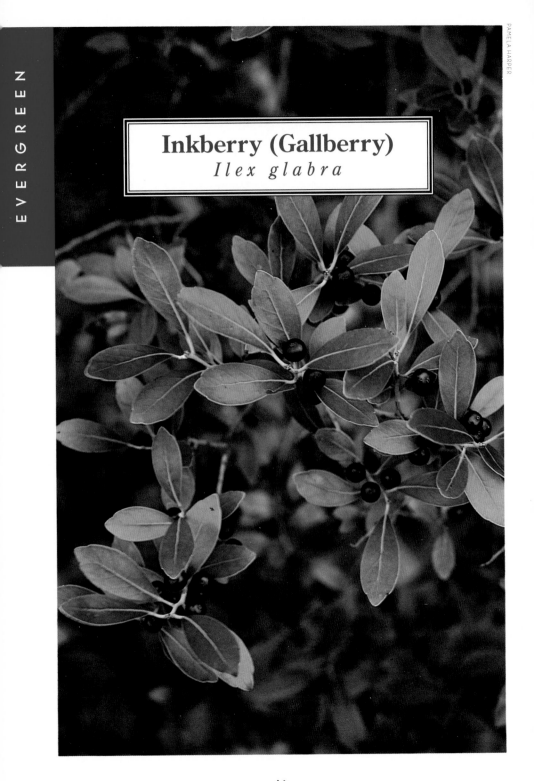

EVERGREEN

Inkberry (Gallberry)
Ilex glabra

Nova Scotia to Florida and west to Texas

5 to 9

OUTSTANDING FEATURES:

Forms an evergreen, nonspiny, stoloniferous shrubby clump, maturing at 8 to 10 feet tall and wider (some cultivars are smaller). Female plants have inconspicuous black fruits.

HABIT AND USE:

The true species plants are useful for masses, naturalistic plantings and hedges. Slower cultivars are often used for foundation plantings.

HOW TO GROW:

Grows well in most ordinary soil conditions except very dry. Tolerates salt spray. Responds well to shearing. Practically pest free. Mulching and fertilizing will pay off.

VARIETIES AND RELATED SPECIES:

'Ivory Queen' — Off-white fruits on a 10-foot-tall bush.

'Compacta' — Also known as 'Princeton Compact'. A fine slower-growing plant, 5 to 6 or more feet tall and wide.

'Chamzin' — Excellent dark green foliage. Slower growing. One of the hardiest selections. May reach 6 feet in height if unpruned.

ELLYN MEYERS

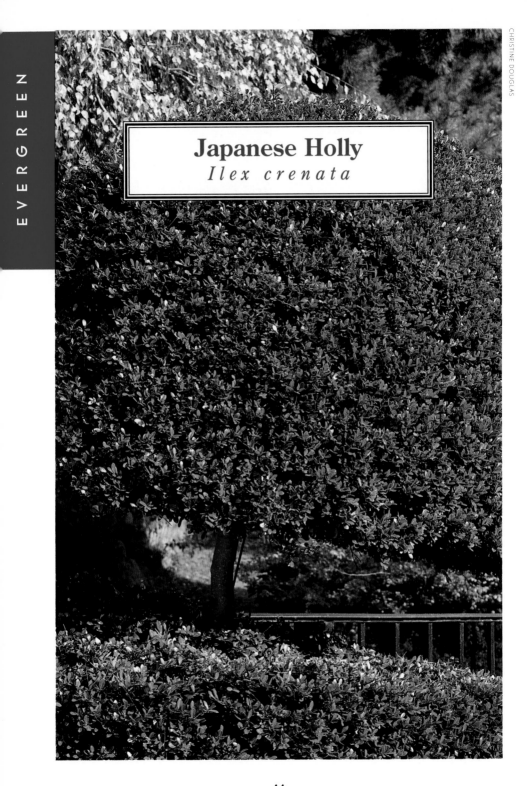

EVERGREEN

Japanese Holly
Ilex crenata

Japan   **6 to 9**

OUTSTANDING FEATURES:

Lustrous, fine-textured evergreen foliage (not spiny) and a multitude of small- to medium-sized shrubby cultivars make Japanese holly popular for landscaping. Small black fruits (on females) are not showy. Collectors may want one of the several cultivars with yellow (really off-white) fruits.

HABIT AND USE:

Rounded, spreading and upright forms are available for use as hedges, foundation plants, topiary and container plants, including bonsai. Marvelously adapted to shearing.

HOW TO GROW:

Adaptable to various soil types. Organic mulch is recommended, especially in Zone 6. Thrives in both sunny and partially shaded situations. Best if shielded from wind in Zone 6, and from afternoon sun in Zones 8 and 9. Use nitrogen fertilizer annually. Spider mites can be a problem, especially in dry weather; daily forceful spraying with plain water is effective.

VARIETIES AND RELATED SPECIES:

Many cultivars exist. A few are:

'Beehive' — A dwarf dense mound, 2-3 feet tall. Male.

'Compacta' — Dark green mound, 5-6 feet. Male.

'Convexa' — An old cultivar, small convex leaves on a compact mound, among the cold hardiest of this group. Often used as a substitute for boxwood. Six feet or taller in time. Female.

'Dwarf Pagoda' — A true dwarf (grows about 2 inches per year). Upright, tiny leaves. Suitable for small gardens and for bonsai. Hardy to Zone 7a. Female.

'Glory' — Hardier than most. Dense globe with tiny leaves, 5 feet tall and 8 feet wide after a dozen years or so. Male.

'Helleri' — Small leaves. Dense plant wider than high, exceeds 3 feet only after many years. Female, but few fruits.

'Highlander' — A dark green, tall plant to 10 feet or more, remarkably cold hardy. Male.

Koehneana Hybrids
Ilex x *koehneana*

Ilex x *koehneana* **'Wirt L. Winn'**

Hybrid   **6b to 9**

PARENTAGE:

aquifolium x *latifolia*

OUTSTANDING FEATURES:

Evergreen trees, potentially 40 feet tall or more, with red fruits.

HABIT AND USE:

The progeny of this cross, *Ilex aquifolium* x *I. latifolia*, are mostly small- to medium-sized, broadly conical trees with evergreen, leathery, dark green, usually spiny leaves 2 to 3-1/2 inches long by about 1-1/4 inches wide. Fruits are large, red and abundant.

HOW TO GROW:

See *Ilex aquifolium* (English Holly).

VARIETIES AND RELATED SPECIES:

'Wirt L. Winn' — Conical form, 20 feet or taller. Large, lustrous, moderately spiny leaves. Good fruit display. Tolerant of heat, drought, and poorly drained soil.

Ilex x *koehneana* **'Ajax'**

CHRISTINE DOUGLAS

Longstalk Holly
Ilex pedunculosa

China and Japan **5 to 8**

OUTSTANDING FEATURES:

Fruits (on female plants) are cherry red and cherrylike on slender stalks up to 1-1/2 inches long, set off by glossy evergreen leaves resembling pear tree foliage. Upright large shrubs, 15 to 20 feet tall in time.

HABIT AND USE:

Much like American holly in shape and size, longstalk holly can be used for similar purposes such as tall hedges and specimen plants. However, because of its rarity and elegance, most are planted as "look-at-me" specimens.

HOW TO GROW:

Similar to American holly, except that longstalk holly is not susceptible to the pests mentioned with regard to American holly.

VARIETIES AND RELATED SPECIES:

None.

Note: Requires a pollinator of the same species.

PATRICIA JOSEPH

Lusterleaf Holly
Ilex latifolia

China and Japan   **8 to 9**

OUTSTANDING FEATURES:

Many people find it hard to believe that a 25-foot tree with leaves 6 inches long and 3 inches wide could be a holly, but such is *Ilex latifolia*. The huge (for holly) leaves are evergreen and coarsely toothed but not spiny, giving the plant the look of southern magnolia but with less messiness on the ground beneath. Dull red fruits are 1/3 inch in diameter in fat clusters on female plants in autumn.

HABIT AND USE:

This species is ideal as small shade or specimen trees. It has been used success-fully in holly breeding, having been a parent of many popular cultivars, including 'Emily Bruner', 'Mary Nell,' 'Wirt L. Winn'.

HOW TO GROW:

Easy to grow in reasonably good soil, sun or partial shade. Mulching and light nitrogen fertilization are recommended.

VARIETIES AND RELATED SPECIES:

See *Ilex cornuta* and *Ilex aquifolium* hybrid cultivars.

PAMELA HARPER

Perny Holly
Ilex pernyi

China   **6b to 9**

OUTSTANDING FEATURES:

Tiny, spiny evergreen leaves sit upright and crowded along stems, with bright red fruits crowded among them, on a narrow upright plant 15 feet tall — truly a collector's item for a prominent spot.

HABIT AND USE:

In addition to being used as an accent, this species has been a good parent in several holly crosses.

HOW TO GROW:

This is not a fussy species, though female plants should have sun for best fruiting, and a bit of pruning now and then will aid shapeliness. Use organic mulch; fertilize annually.

VARIETIES AND RELATED SPECIES:

See *Ilex cornuta* hybrid cultivars; also *I.* x *aquipernyi.*

PAMELA HARPER

Topel Holly
Ilex x *attenuata*

Ilex x *attenuata* '**Foster #2**'

Southeastern United States   **6b to 9**

PARENTAGE:

cassine x *opaca*

OUTSTANDING FEATURES:

This handsome group of hybrid evergreen hollies has narrow, bright green leaves with slightly spiny margins. Dark red fruits last all winter. Grows 20 to 25 feet tall.

HABIT AND USE:

Fine-textured, slender conical form makes these hybrids useful for specimens, corner plantings and screens.

HOW TO GROW:

Good soil, full sun and gentle pruning give best results. See American Holly. Relatively pest free.

VARIETIES AND RELATED SPECIES:

'Foster #2' — Excellent foliage, lots of red fruits. 20 feet tall or more. Hardy in Zone 6b.

'Foster #4' — A good male for pollen. Zone 6b.

'East Palatka' — A popular holly with larger fruits and leaves than those of the Fosters, but cold hardy only to Zone 7a. Leaves are essentially spineless.

'Aurantiaca' — Has great masses of large orange fruit.

'Bright Horizon' — A compact plant, 6 feet tall and 2-1/2 feet wide after 12 years. Large (1/2 inch) red fruits.

'Cacapon' — Grows to 8 feet tall. Crinkled, dark green leaves and plenty of dark red fruits.

'Earlibright' — Produces early, orange-red fruits. An upright plant, about 7 feet tall and half as wide.

'Jackson' — A male pollinator for many northern female cultivars. Good foliage. Narrow upright plant to 10 feet tall.

'Red Sprite' — Also known as 'Nana' and 'Compacta'. Compact slow grower to 5 feet tall with large red fruits.

'Simpson's Early Male' — Pollinator for southern-type females.

'Stop Light' — Formerly 'Hopperton'. Good foliage, large half-inch berries, light gray stems.

'Sunset' — Large, dark green leaves to 6 inches. Spreading bush becoming 6 feet high and 8 feet wide. Abundant reddish orange fruits.

'Winter Red' — A wonderful cultivar, 8 feet tall after many years. Lustrous dark green foliage. Abundant and persistent rich red fruits. Cut twigs stay beautiful for months indoors without water.

Yaupon Holly
Ilex vomitoria

Ilex vomitoria **'Pendula'**

Southeastern United States   **7b to 9**

OUTSTANDING FEATURES:

Small but shiny and translucent fruits and glossy, dark green evergreen leaves of modest size (1/2 to 1-1/2 inches long, half as wide). Attractive gray-white bark. Picturesque informal shrubs or small trees 15 to 20 feet tall. Medium to fast growth rate.

HABIT AND USE:

Yaupons are versatile, serving well as specimens, foundation plantings, hedges, screens, backdrops for smaller plants, mass plantings, wall plants, espaliers and topiary. There are dwarf, upright and weeping forms.

HOW TO GROW:

Easy to transplant, drought and heat resistant. Will grow in soils from alkaline to acidic and from dry to swampy. Tolerant of salt spray. Use organic mulch. Easy-does-it with nitrogen fertilization and pruning (shear for formal hedges only). Free from pest and disease problems. Yaupons are dream plants.

VARIETIES AND RELATED SPECIES:

'Folsom's Weeping' — A small tree with long pendulous branches and red fruits. Similar plants are 'Gray's Weeping' and 'Pendula'. Both male and female weeping forms are available.

'Gray's Greenleaf' — An upright spreading small tree with red fruits.

'Jewel' — A medium to large shrub with horizontal branching, red fruits and attractive gray stems.

'Nana' — One of several low-growing cultivars easily kept at 3- to 5-foot height for many years with light pruning. Similar cultivars ('Compacta', 'Schillings Dwarf' and 'Stokes Dwarf') are often confused in the nursery trade.

'Shadow's Female' — A large shrub or small tree with large, dark green leaves and red fruits. More cold hardy than many other cultivars (Zone 7a).

'Yellow Berry' — A cultivar with yellow fruits; others are 'Wiggins Yellow' and 'Yawkey'.

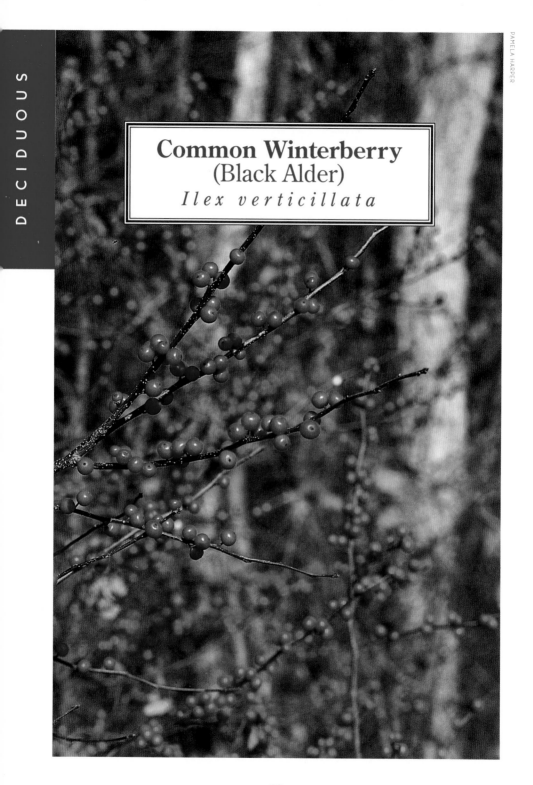

DECIDUOUS

Common Winterberry
(Black Alder)
Ilex verticillata

Nova Scotia and New England, west to Minnesota and south to Florida and Texas

4 to 9a

OUTSTANDING FEATURES:

Deciduous shrubs of varying characteristics, from 4 to 15 feet tall. Females bear fruits 1/4 inch or larger in shades of red and orange, rarely yellow. Most experts agree this species includes "northern" and "southern" types. Northern types have many light brown stems, smallish leaves and a moderate growth rate. They bloom 2 to 3 weeks later than the southern types. Southern plants have larger, thicker leaves, darker stems and more open and faster growth. For pollination, females need males from the same geographic group.

HABIT AND USE:

Cultivars offer a range of shrubby plants, from small to large, for foundations, corners, borders, screens and naturalizing, and for cut branches that hold their "berries" beautifully indoors without water. They also make good specimen plants. To attract birds, plant red-fruited cultivars rather than orange or yellow ones.

HOW TO GROW:

Growth is best in moist, water-retentive soil (muck, clay, clay-loam), slightly acidic, in full sun. Some cultivars are drought-tolerant; most will benefit from irrigation during dry spells. All will respond well to organic mulch over root zones.

VARIETIES AND RELATED SPECIES:

N = northern type; S = southern

'Afterglow' — N. A compact shrub, 10 feet high and wide after 30 years. Glossy green leaves, plentiful orange-red fruits. One of the cold hardier selections.

'Aurantiaca' — N. Great masses of large orange fruit on a smallish bush.

'Bright Horizon' — S. Herringbone branching on a compact plant, 6 feet tall and 2 1/2 feet wide after 12 years. Large red fruits.

'Cacapon' — N. Grows to 8 feet tall. Crinkled dark green leaves, plenty of dark red fruits.

'Earlibright' — N. An early fruiting, upright plant about 7 feet tall and half as wide. Fruits are orange-red.

'Stop Light' (formerly 'Hopperton') — N. Good foliage, large berries, light gray stems.

'Jackson' — N. A male pollinator for many northern female cultivars. Good foliage. Narrow upright plant to 10 feet tall.

'Red Sprite' (aka 'Nana' and 'Compacta') — N. Compact, slow grower to 5 feet with large red fruits.

'Simpson's Early Male' — S. Midseason to late pollinator for southern-type females.

'Sunset' — S. Large dark green leaves to 6 inches. Spreading bush becoming 6 feet high and 8 feet wide. Abundant reddish orange fruits.

'Winter Red' — S. A marvelous cultivar, 8 feet tall after many years. Lustrous dark green foliage. Its rich red fruits are abundant and very persistent. Cut twigs stay beautiful for months indoors without water.

Japanese Winterberry
(Finetooth Holly)
Ilex serrata

Japan and China   **5b (or 6) to 8.**

OUTSTANDING FEATURES:

A deciduous shrubby species of fine texture, 10 to 15 feet tall. Female plants have profuse displays of small red fruits (3/16 inch across, rarely white or yellow) if an *I. serrata* male is nearby. The fruits appear in late summer before leaves drop and persist for some time.

HABIT AND USE:

These medium to large rounded shrubs are good for naturalizing and massing, and cut branches are great for arrangements. Horticulturists have crossed this species with *Ilex verticillata,* producing some notable cultivars.

HOW TO GROW:

Best in moist sites, sunny or partially shady. Use organic mulch generously, about 3 inches thick. Fertilize annually.

VARIETIES AND RELATED SPECIES:

Few cultivars exist in commerce, though some may be seen at U. S. National Arboretum and some other public gardens.

Ilex serrata **'Sundrops'**

Possumhaw

Ilex decidua

Ilex decidua **'Warren Red'**

Maryland to central Illinois, south to Florida and Texas

5b to 9a

OUTSTANDING FEATURES:

Considered by some the showiest of all native deciduous hollies, this species is a vigorous large shrub or small tree (as tall as 25 feet or more) with rich, glossy green foliage and profusions of glossy fruits from deep red to orange and (rarely) yellow. Stems are usually light gray and attractive, especially in winter. Pollination of female plants is by males of the species, or by males of *Ilex opaca* (American Holly) which bloom at the same time.

HABIT AND USE:

This species is adaptable to pruning into small trees with single or several trunks. Large shrub forms (not tree-trained) are effective for screens, background plantings and naturalizing. The fruits and light gray bark are particularly lovely against a backdrop of needled evergreens.

HOW TO GROW:

Adapts well to a wide range of soil conditions, except high alkalinity. See common winterberry.

VARIETIES AND RELATED SPECIES

'Council Fire' — A sturdy rounded large shrub to 15 feet tall with dark green leaves and plentiful dark red fruits.

'Pocahontas' — Abundant large red fruit cover the silvery gray branches of this 16-foot upright small tree.

'Red Cascade' — Large shrub to 15 feet or more with broad, glossy green leaves, large persistent red fruits and silvery white bark.

'Red Escort' — A male for pollinating. Dense, vigorous, large shrub with excellent foliage.

'Warren Red' — A broad arching form to 18 feet or more, with great quantities of shiny red fruit and lustrous dark green foliage. An outstanding cultivar.

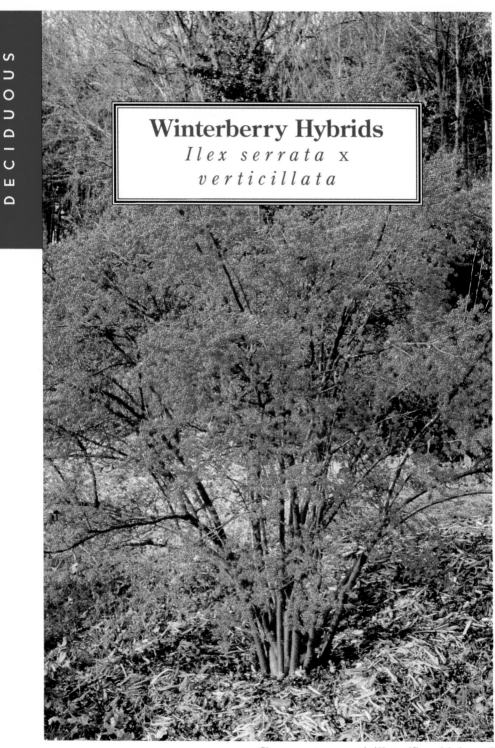

Winterberry Hybrids
Ilex serrata x *verticillata*

Ilex serrata **x** *verticillata* **'Sparkleberry'**

Hybrid   **5 to 8**

OUTSTANDING FEATURES:

Vigorous, slender-branched deciduous shrubs from 8 feet to 12 feet tall with attractive foliage. Females bear vivid red fruits in abundance before and after leaf drop, providing spectacular displays.

HABIT AND USE:

Named selections are useful in masses, bank plantings, mixed or monocultural borders and backdrops for smaller plants.

HOW TO GROW:

Site requirements and cultural tips are similar to those for *Ilex verticillata* (common winterberry). Pruning in early spring before new growth will control size and increase compactness without diminishing fruiting.

VARIETIES AND RELATED SPECIES:

'Apollo' — A fine consistent pollinator (male).
'Bonfire' — Vigorous, spreading form, 10 feet high or more at maturity, loaded with scarlet-red fruits.
'Harvest Red' — Deep red fruits hold color exceptionally well on a bush maturing at 12 feet.
'Sparkleberry' — A vigorous, upright plant 10 to 12 feet tall with brilliant red fruits that last all winter.

Ilex **'Sparkleberry'**

Recommended Hollies
by Region

Northeast

(primarily coastal areas)

Ilex opaca — American holly, hardy cultivars
Ilex x *meserveae* — Blue holly
Ilex glabra — Inkberry
Ilex pedunculosa — Longstalk holly
Ilex verticillata — Common winterberry
Ilex pernyi — Perny holly

Ilex opaca

Ilex x *meserveae*

M id-Atlantic

Ilex aquifolium — English holly
Ilex x *altaclerensis*— Highclere holly
Ilex aquifolium x *cornuta,* 'Nellie R. Stevens'
Ilex crenata — Japanese holly
Ilex glabra — Inkberry
Ilex x *meserveae* — Blue holly
Ilex opaca — American holly
Ilex serrata x *verticillata* — Winterberry hybrids

Ilex aquifolium

Ilex x *altaclerensis*

S outheast

Ilex opaca — American holly
Ilex crenata — Japanese holly
Ilex cornuta — Chinese holly
Ilex vomitoria — Yaupon holly
Ilex x *attenuata* — Topel holly
Ilex x *aquipernyi* — Aquipern holly
Ilex aquifolium x *cornuta* 'Nellie R. Stevens'
Ilex decidua — Possumhaw
Ilex verticillata — Common winterberry
Ilex serrata x *verticillata* — Winterberry hybrids

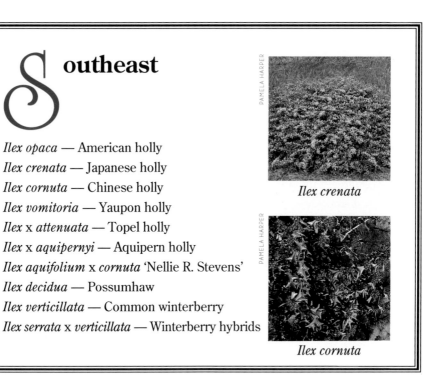

Ilex crenata

Ilex cornuta

L ower South

(Zone 9, not 10)

Ilex x *altaclerensis* — Highclere holly
Ilex x *koehneana,* 'Wirt L. Winn' —
               Koehneana hybrid
Ilex x *attenuata* 'East Palatka' — Topel holly
Ilex vomitoria — Yaupon holly
Ilex cornuta — Chinese holly

Ilex x *koehneana*

Ilex x *attenuata*

M idwest

Ilex opaca — American holly
Ilex pedunculosa — Longstalk holly
Ilex glabra — Inkberry
Ilex x *meserveae* — Blue holly
Ilex crenata — Japanese holly (in warmer
portions of Midwest)
Ilex decidua — Possumhaw
Ilex verticillata — Common winterberry
Ilex serrata x *verticillata* — Winterberry hybrids

Ilex pedunculosa

Ilex glabra

Central Plains

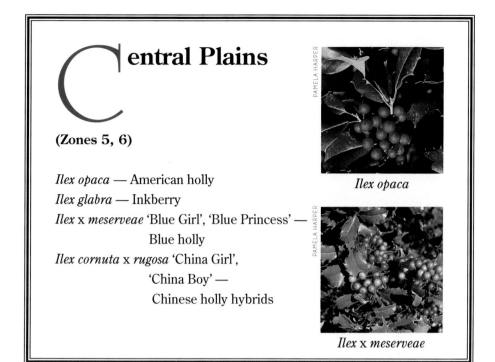

(Zones 5, 6)

Ilex opaca — American holly
Ilex glabra — Inkberry
Ilex x *meserveae* 'Blue Girl', 'Blue Princess' —
        Blue holly
Ilex cornuta x *rugosa* 'China Girl',
          'China Boy' —
            Chinese holly hybrids

Ilex opaca

Ilex x *meserveae*

Rocky Mountains

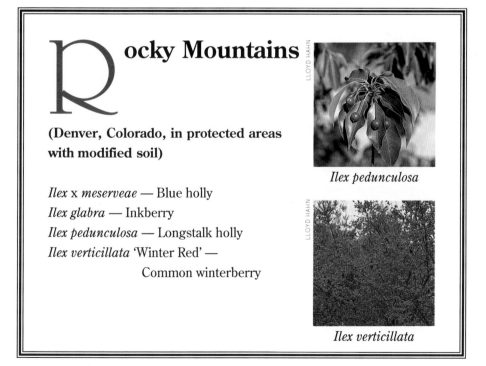

**(Denver, Colorado, in protected areas
with modified soil)**

Ilex x *meserveae* — Blue holly
Ilex glabra — Inkberry
Ilex pedunculosa — Longstalk holly
Ilex verticillata 'Winter Red' —
          Common winterberry

Ilex pedunculosa

Ilex verticillata

West Coast

(California)

Ilex cornuta 'Berries Jubilee', 'Burfordii',
         'Dwarf Burford' —
         Chinese holly
Ilex crenata 'Compacta' — Japanese holly
Ilex vomitoria 'Nana', 'Stokes Dwarf' —
         Yaupon holly
Ilex x *aquipernyi* 'San Jose' — Aquipern holly

Ilex crenata

Ilex x *aquipernyi*

Pacific Northwest

Ilex aquifolium — English holly
Ilex x *meserveae* — Blue holly
Ilex crenata — Japanese holly
Ilex pedunculosa — Longstalk holly
Ilex x *aquipernyi* 'San Jose' — Aquipern holly
Ilex decidua — Possumhaw
Ilex verticillata — Common winterberry

Ilex aquifolium

Ilex verticillata

HARDINESS ZONE

Map

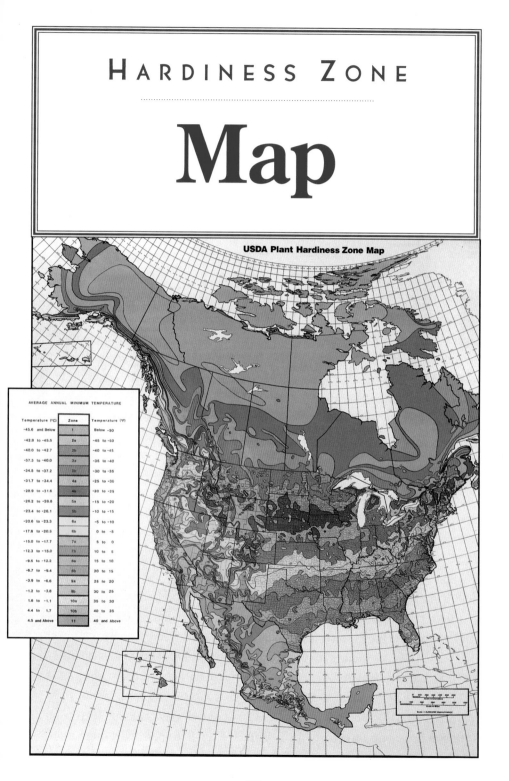

USDA Plant Hardiness Zone Map

AVERAGE ANNUAL MINIMUM TEMPERATURE

Temperature (°C)	Zone	Temperature (°F)
-45.6 and Below	1	Below -50
-42.8 to -45.5	2a	-45 to -50
-40.0 to -42.7	2b	-40 to -45
-37.3 to -40.0	3a	-35 to -40
-34.5 to -37.2	3b	-30 to -35
-31.7 to -34.4	4a	-25 to -30
-28.9 to -31.6	4b	-20 to -25
-26.2 to -28.8	5a	-15 to -20
-23.4 to -26.1	5b	-10 to -15
-20.6 to -23.3	6a	-5 to -10
-17.8 to -20.5	6b	0 to -5
-15.0 to -17.7	7a	5 to 0
-12.3 to -15.0	7b	10 to 5
-9.5 to -12.2	8a	15 to 10
-6.7 to -9.4	8b	20 to 15
-3.9 to -6.6	9a	25 to 20
-1.2 to -3.8	9b	30 to 25
1.6 to -1.1	10a	35 to 30
4.4 to 1.7	10b	40 to 35
4.5 and Above	11	40 and Above

WHERE TO FIND IT

If you travel, have babies or shoot pool, you likely enjoy exchanging experiences and information with others who do the same.

If you grow hollies, or at least enjoy seeing hollies, then surely you will want to meet other holly people, and receive printed material with holly information. Holly Society of America offers regular national and regional meetings and produces a quarterly *Holly Society Journal* and other publications devoted to holly. For information, write or call: Linda R. Parsons, Secretary, **HOLLY SOCIETY OF AMERICA,** 11318 West Murdock, Witchita, KS 67212-6609; (316) 721-5668.

SOURCES OF HOLLY

Holly Society of America maintains a list of more than 50 sources for some 400 species, hybrids and cultivars. The list indicates whether nurseries are wholesale or retail, and whether the latter will ship plants. The source list costs $2 and is available from Linda R. Parsons, Secretary of HSA, 11318 West Murdock, Witchita, KS 67212-6609, or from C. L. Dickinson, HSA, 37 Blackjack Rd., Hendersonville, NC 28739.

Members of the Holly Society are famously generous with cuttings, and sometimes plants. A popular event at annual meetings of HSA is the "Holly Exchange Program." Members bring cuttings of their favorite hollies to share.

HOLLY PLACES

Official holly arboreta and test tenters are wonderful places for viewing and enjoying hollies. Send a stamped, self-addressed envelope to Publications Department, Brooklyn Botanic Garden, 1000 Washington Ave., Brooklyn, NY 11225, Attention: Official Holly Arboreta and Test Centers.

Some public parks in east-coastal and east-mountainous states feature native hollies in native habitats. Travel bureaus can help you find them.

Two spectacular native forests of primarily American holly, *Ilex opaca*, are Sunken Forest at the Fire Island National Seashore, reached by ferry from Sayville, Long Island, NY; and Sandy Hook Park on the seacoast of Monmouth County, NJ.

Information about Sunken Forest, which also harbors inkberry, *Ilex glabra*, and other native trees and shrubs, is available from Sailors Haven Visitors Information, (516) 597-8980. Sandy Hook, part of Gateway National Recreation Area, is a peninsula jutting into the Atlantic Ocean. It is open daily; there is an admission charge from Memorial Day to Labor Day.